# MEDEA

Euripides

# Prestwick House

## LITERARY TOUCHSTONE CLASSICS™

P.O. Box 658 Clayton, Delaware 19938 • www.prestwickhouse.com

SENIOR EDITOR: Paul Moliken

EDITOR: Darlene Gilmore

TRANSLATOR: J.E. Thomas

COVER DESIGN: Maria J. Mendoza

PRODUCTION: Dana Kerr

# Prestwick House
## LITERARY TOUCHSTONE CLASSICS™

P.O. Box 658 • CLAYTON, DELAWARE 19938
TEL: 1.800.932.4593
FAX: 1.888.718.9333
WEB: www.prestwickhouse.com

Prestwick House Teaching Units,™ Activity Packs,™ and Response Journals™ are the perfect complement for these editions. To purchase teaching resources for this book, visit www.prestwickhouse.com.

*Performance Note*

Professionals and amateurs, please note that *Medea* translated by J. E. Thomas is fully protected under the copyright laws of the United States and all countries within the copyright union. Performance rights are hereby granted for non-profit educational purposes. Performance rights for any for-profit purposes are reserved by the publisher. All inquiries related to obtaining performance rights and royalty rates should be directed to Prestwick House, Inc.  P.O. Box 658 Clayton, DE 19938.

# CONTENTS

# NOTES

**What is a literary classic and why are these classic works important to the world?**

A literary classic is a work of the highest excellence that has something important to say about life and/or the human condition and says it with great artistry. A classic, through its enduring presence, has withstood the test of time and is not bound by time, place, or customs. It speaks to us today as forcefully as it spoke to people one hundred or more years ago, and as forcefully as it will speak to people of future generations. For this reason, a classic is said to have universality.

*Medea* has meaning in our time because it raises such difficult and disturbing issues. As a barbarian, woman, and witch, Medea is instantly set apart from her community; she is isolated in almost every possible way. Surprisingly, this helps to make her a heroic figure; alone and without aid, she must do everything for herself, in spite of the challenges set against her. She defies the odds and is victorious over her enemies—yet at the end of the play, the audience is far from unanimously on her side. Medea's single-minded devotion to revenge and the horrible things she does to achieve it vitiate the sympathy she would receive. She has just grievances against Jason and Creon, who have been unjust to her. Her actions, however, are shocking and defy the most basic laws and assumptions of human society. Thus, Euripides questions what it means to be a hero, as well as what it means to be a good person and part of a community.

After reading this play, look at the motives and actions of all its characters and see if you can find any truly sympathetic figures. Does anyone deserve what they get? And, if Medea's actions are so truly heinous, why does Euripides elevate her so much at the end of the play, when she is almost a goddess? These are not easy questions to answer, and they point to why Euripides has been one of the most successful psychological dramatists of all time, a poet whose works continue to shock and confound audiences and readers almost 2,500 years after they were written.

# Translator's Note

In preparing this edition, I have for the most part followed the Oxford text of Diggle. Like most Greek texts, there are many areas of confusion in the manuscripts of *Medea*; I have tried to stay as close to the Greek as possible, but my primary concern was to produce a coherent English text for a young audience uninterested in the cruces of palaeography and papyrology. I also used the Cambridge commentary of Donald Mastronarde and followed many of his emendations to aid in producing a smooth final product.

J. E. Thomas
Providence, R.I.

**Reading Pointers for Sharper Insights**

As you read *Medea*, be aware of the following themes and elements:

- **Greeks vs. Barbarians**: In the 5th century, the area of modern Greece was occupied by dozens of small city-states and islands, each with its own peculiar legal and cultural institutions. Although these people were tied together by similar religious practices and often made alliances with one another, there was no unified Greek organization—no country of Greece. Hence, the Greeks viewed the world through a linguistic distinction: Greek-speakers, despite all their differences, were viewed as civilized, rational people, while anyone who did not speak Greek was termed a barbarian. The word *barbaros* had fewer negative connotations for the Greeks than it has for us, but the Greeks still viewed themselves as culturally superior and more enlightened than even the best of barbarians. They applied this designation without exception; all non-Greek speakers—the nomadic Scythians of modern Ukraine, the inhabitants of the powerful, cosmopolitan Persian Empire, even the Romans—were ultimately, in Greek eyes, just barbarians.

  This distinction is very important in the play, because Medea is a barbarian and all the other characters are Greek. This makes Medea instantly an outsider, and for the Greeks, ties to homeland and community were very, very strong.

- **Gender**: A second important distinction is obvious: Medea is a woman. In ancient Athens, women of well-born families were expected to stay at home in specially designated women's quarters *all the time*, except during certain religious festivals. Marriages were arranged by a girl's father or guardian. Women were not true citizens of the democracy and could not speak or vote in the assembly. They were not even allowed to speak in court, a basic right for Athenian men. As a woman and barbarian, Medea is very alienated. She, however, thinks of herself as Jason's equal; she refuses to be a submissive wife, which has disastrous results for her entire family and herself. Her manipulation of rhetoric is an especially masculine characteristic for the Greeks; by the play's end, she has essentially manipulated herself—her revenge destroys her as well as her enemies. Note throughout the play the emphasis Medea puts on her marriage with Jason, in which her father was completely uninvolved. She herself contracted the marriage and views her relationship with Jason as a friendship, one which he consistently violates by refusing to see her as his equal. Euripides was sometimes considered a misogynist by the Athenians because he wrote female characters like Medea, who defy everything the (male) Athenians thought a woman should be. Do you agree? Is Medea a good role model for women?

- **Witchcraft**: Finally, Medea is a witch. While Euripides downplays this aspect of her life, the Athenian audience would know it already, and the poisoned clothing Medea uses to kill Creon and the princess has strong overtones of witchcraft. Witches, according to Greek thought, operated mainly via poison and drugs—just think of our concept of the witch's brew. They could also turn to specific deities for help. Certain gods in the Greek pantheon, like Hecate, goddess of the crossroads, were considered dark and evil and more suited to witchcraft and sorcery than to proper religion; such gods were usually invoked by people plotting wicked deeds.

  Keep in mind that normal Greek religion included many aspects that seem similar to witchcraft to us—curses, prophecy and fortune-telling, animal sacrifice and rites involving the blood and entrails of the sacrificed victim. Greek witchcraft differed from this religion in the types and uses of ceremonies it employed.

## SETTING

In front of Medea's house in Corinth. There is an entrance onto the stage from the house, as well as two side entrances leading toward the palace and toward the main road away from the city.

# Dramatis Personae
*(in order of appearance)*

Nurse, *aged servant of Medea*

Tutor *to the children of Jason and Medea*

Medea, *formerly princess of Colchis, now wife of Jason*

Chorus *of the women of Corinth*

Creon, *king of Corinth*

Jason, *hero and captain of the Argo, husband of Medea*

Aegeus, *king of Athens*

Messenger

Children of Medea

various unnamed attendants, servants, and guards

# MEDEA

*[Enter Nurse from the house.]*

*Nurse*

If only the ship Argo[1] had never flown
through the dark Symplegades[2] into the land
of Colchis,[3] and the felled pine had never
fallen in the glens of Pelion,[4]

5    and the hands of heroes never manned its oars,
never sought the Golden Fleece for Pelias![5]
Then my mistress Medea would not have sailed
to the towers of Iolcus,[6] her heart smitten
by love for Jason.  Then she would never

10   have persuaded the daughters of Pelias
to kill their father, and been forced to live
in this land of Corinth with her husband
and children, an exile who pleased the citizens
of her new home, a help to Jason himself

15   in all matters.  This is the greatest salvation,
when a wife stands together with her husband.
But, now it's all hate, what was dearest is sick,
for Jason betrayed his children and my mistress
and goes to bed with a royal marriage:

20   he's married the child of Creon who rules this land.
Poor, dishonored Medea shouts oaths

[1] *the first ship; see Mythology (page 64)*

[2] *the cliffs that formed the entrance to the Black Sea*

[3] *the city on the Black Sea where Medea's father was king*

[4] *the mountain where the Argo was built*

[5] *Jason's uncle*

[6] *the city where Pelias ruled*

[7]Normally, the
groom shook
hands with the
bride's father.
Medea's active
participation
in the wedding
shows that she is
more than an ordi-
nary woman and
considers herself
Jason's equal.

and recalls the great faith of their right hands[7]
and calls the gods to witness the sort of return
she gets from Jason.  She lies, fasting,
25    surrendering her body to pain,
wasting away in tears ever since she perceived
herself mistreated by her husband,
neither lifting her eyes nor moving her face
from the ground; when she hears her friends rebuke
        her,
30    she listens like a rock or the sea's wave,
except when she turns her white face away
and groans to herself for her dear father
and her land and the home she betrayed and left
with a husband who now dishonors her.
35    The poor thing has been taught by misfortune
the importance of not losing your homeland.
She hates her children and hates the sight of them,
and I fear that she's plotting something new.
It'll only bring her greater suffering,
40    for she is terrible; no one takes her on
as an enemy and emerges the victor.
The children are coming! They've stopped
        exercising—
they don't understand their mother's trouble,
45    for a young mind doesn't like to worry.

[Enter Tutor with Children from offstage.]

Tutor

Long-time possession of my mistress,
why do you stand by the gates, in solitude,
bewailing your troubles to yourself?
Does Medea wish to be alone without you?

Nurse

50    Old attendant of the children of Jason,
for the best slaves, the affairs of their masters,
going badly, affect even their own wits.
I have gone so far into pain that desire
took me to come here and tell the sky
55    and the earth of my mistress' affairs.

*Tutor*

    So the poor woman has not stopped groaning?

*Nurse*

    I envy you:  her suffering's only started.

*Tutor*

    Fool—if one may say this of one's master.
    How little she knows of her new troubles.

*Nurse*

60    What is it, old man?  Don't keep it from me.

*Tutor*

    No, I regret even what I've just said.

*Nurse*

    Please, don't conceal it from your fellow slave,
    for I'll be silent around here, if I must.

*Tutor*

    I was near the dice games, where the old men
65    sit, around the holy spring of Pirene,[8]
    and I heard someone say, when I didn't
    seem to be listening, that Creon,
    the ruler of this land, intends to drive
    these children from Corinthian earth
70    with their mother.  I don't know if the story
    is sound, although I hope it isn't.

*Nurse*

    And Jason will allow his children to suffer,
    even if he quarrels with their mother?

*Tutor*

    Old things are abandoned for the new in-laws,
75    and that man is not a friend to this house.

*Nurse*

    We're done for, if we add this new trouble
    to the old one, before we've suffered it.

[8]*in the center of Corinth*

*Tutor*

But, you, since it's not the right time for our mistress
to know this, keep quiet and tell no one.

*Nurse*

80    Children, do you hear how your father acts towards
          you?
      I won't wish him death, for he's still my master,
      but he has proven bad to his friends.

*Tutor*

      What mortal isn't?  Do you learn this now?
85    Every single person loves himself
      more than his fellow man, if a father
      does not love his children because of his bed.

*Nurse*

      Go inside now, children, it will be all right—
      but you, isolate them as much as you can,
90    keep them away from their mother while she's angry.
      I've already seen her looking at them
      like a bull, like she was about to do
      something; and she won't stop her anger,
      I know for certain, before she has fallen
95    on someone.  I just hope she does it to
      enemies, at least, and not to friends.

*Medea*[9]                              *[from within the house*[10]*]*
      Oh!
      I am miserable, unhappy in my labors!
      Oh me, I wish I were dead.

*Nurse*

      This is it, dear children; your mother
100   stirs her heart, stirs her anger.
      Hurry quickly inside the house,
      and don't go within her sight.
      Don't go near her, but watch out
      for her fierce heart and the hateful nature
105   of her contumacious mind.

[9]*The meter\* Euripides uses here shows Medea's heightened emotion; the Nurse responds to her in the same meter, as if infected by the emotion.*

[10]*Greek tragedies often feature lines spoken by a character within the house and heard by those outside.*

\*Terms marked in the text with (\*) can be looked up in the Glossary
for additional information.

Go now, get inside quickly!
It is clear she will soon light
with greater spirit the cloud
of lamentation now rising
110 in its beginning. Whatever will
her heart, bitten by troubles,
high-spirited, hard to check, do?

*Medea*
Alas!
I have suffered, oh, dreadfully
115 have I suffered things
worthy of lamentation.
Oh, let them die, the accursed children
of a hateful mother, with their father,
and let the whole house disappear!

*Nurse*
120 Oh my, the poor woman!
Why do you give the boys a share
of their father's embraces? Why do you hate them?
Alas, children, how I fear you will suffer!
Royal tempers are terrible—it seems that
125 they rule much, but are themselves rarely ruled,
and with difficulty do they control their anger.
It is better to live always among equals;
for myself, at any rate, I hope
to grow old securely in modest circumstances.
130 First of all, the very idea of moderation
wins first prize in speaking, and in action,
is by far the best way for mortals, but excessive power
can produce no proper return for human beings,
instead giving back greater madness
135 whenever God is angry at the house.

[*The Chorus marches in from offstage, chanting.*[11]]

*Chorus*
I heard the voice, and I heard the cry
of the unhappy woman of Colchis.

[11]*see* Conventions
of Greek Drama
(*page 69*)

Is she not yet calm?  Tell me, old woman.
For I heard her moaning within the
140    double-gated hall, nor am I pleased, lady,
by the woes of the house,
since friendship has been mixed for me.

*Nurse*

The house is undone; all this is ruined;
for a royal marriage has taken the master,
145    and the mistress wastes away her life in
her chamber, allowing no friends to speak
words of comfort to her mind.

*Medea*

Alas!
If only a lightning bolt from heaven would go
150    through my head!  What good does it do me to remain
alive?
Oh, oh!  I wish I could cast off
this hateful life and take my rest in death!

*Chorus*

Strophe[12]

O Zeus[13] and Earth and Light,
155    did you hear the cry
the unhappy woman utters?
What is this desire for the terrible
bed of rest, foolish woman?
You would hasten the end of death?
160    Do not pray for this!
If your husband gives himself to a new bed,
do not be angry at him for this;
Zeus will be your advocate in it.
Do not pine excessively, mourning your husband.

*Medea*

O great Themis[14] and lady Artemis,[15]
165    do you see what I suffer, having bound
my cursed husband with holy
oaths?  I wish I could see him and his bride

[12]*The songs and choral odes of Greek tragedy usually take the form of metrically matched stanzas called the strophe and its counterpart, the antistrophe. Sometimes, the ode will end with a single, unmatched stanza, called the epode. These verses are sung in lyric meters, and the Chorus dances in accompaniment.*

[13]*the king of the gods*

[14]*the goddess of justice/what's right*

[15]*Although normally mentioned as goddess of the hunt or of childbirth, Artemis is here called upon as a general protector of women.*

and the whole house violently destroyed!
What injustices they dared to commit, unprovoked,
170        against me!
O father, O city, from whom I was parted,
after I shamefully killed my own brother![16]

[16]*See page 64*

*Nurse*

Do you hear how she speaks and calls upon
Themis of Prayers and Zeus, who
175    dispenses and rules mortal oaths?
There is no way my mistress will stop
her anger in some small act.

*Chorus*

*Antistrophe*

I wish she would come out
into our sight and accept
180        the sound of spoken words,
if somehow she might put aside her deep-hearted
anger and the passion of her mind.
Let my eager goodwill not be
absent for my friends.
185    But go inside now and bring her out
of the house  Tell her we come as friends,
make haste before she does something bad
to those within, for this sorrow will set something
great in motion.

*Nurse*

190    I will do this, but I fear I won't persuade
my mistress.
Still, I will do it as a favor to you.
Although to her maids, her gaze
is like a bull's, like a lioness guarding her young,
195    whenever one draws near, bringing some report.
You wouldn't be mistaken if you said
the men of the past were unlucky and completely stupid
who invented songs for good times,
for banquets and dinner parties,
200    as delightful things to hear,

but no human being has found a way to
stop with music and many-toned songs
hateful grief, from which death
and terrible chance overthrow houses.
205 It would be a real benefit for humanity
to cure these things with songs, but at
banquets with good meals, why make your voice shrill
in vain?
The fullness of the feast at hand
210 holds joy for mortals in and of itself.

*[Exit Nurse into the house.]*

*Chorus*

*Epode*

I hear her voice groaning and moaning,
 shouting shrill cries of grief
 at the evil bridegroom who betrayed her bed.
Having suffered injustice she calls on the gods,
215  on Zeus's Themis, guardian of oaths,
 who made her come to Greece
 across the strait,
 through the sea at night
 near the salt-enclosure of impenetrable Pontus.

*[Enter Medea from the house.]*

*Medea*

220 Women of Corinth, I came out of the house
so that you would not reproach me. I know
that many people are seen as haughty,
some in private, others among people.
Others, however, from living quietly
225 get a bad reputation for laziness.
It's not justice in men's eyes, when they hate a man
before learning his true character clearly,
when they've only seen him and suffered
no injustice from him.  A foreigner,
230 especially, ought to make concessions
to the city, and I would not praise even

one native-born who is conceited and
bitter to his fellow citizens because
of ignorance. This unexpected problem
235   that falls on me has destroyed my soul;
I am ruined; I have lost the pleasure of life—
I want to die, friends, for the one who was
everything to me (I've learned it well enough),
my husband, has turned out to be the worst of men.
240   Of all things that live and have intelligence,
we women are the most wretched creatures.
First, we must buy a husband at a high price[17]
and take a master over our bodies,[18]
an even more painful evil than the other.
245   Here the stakes are highest: do we take
a bad man or a good one? A woman can't
get divorced and keep her good reputation,
and she has no right to refuse her husband.
After arriving among new customs and rules,
250   she must be a prophet, since she was not
taught at home how to deal with her husband.
If we work hard at this, and our husband
bears the yoke of marriage without violence,
life is enviable; but, if not,
255   better to die.  A man, when he is annoyed
with those inside, goes out and stops the nausea
in his heart, but we must look to just one person.[19]
They say that we live lives free from danger,
while they go out to fight wars with spears,
260   but their logic is flawed. I would rather
stand shield to shield three times than give birth just
        once.[20]
But here is the real point for you and me:
This is your city, here you have your father's
265   home and your life's enjoyment and your friends,
but I have been outraged by my husband
and am alone, without city, carried off
from a barbarian land, with no mother,
no brother, no relative to whom I could sail,
270   away from this disaster. Therefore,
I would ask of you only this: if I

[17]*a reference to the practice of giving a dowry with a bride*

[18]*Greek women, especially in Athens, had very few legal rights and always had to be represented by a guardian, normally the father or husband.*

[19]*Respectable Athenian women were expected to stay inside their homes most of the time, having very little contact with the outside world except during religious festivals.*

[20]*Childbirth was very dangerous for Greek women, given the medical knowledge of the day. For a woman to die in childbirth was roughly analogous to a man dying in battle—she had died fulfilling her duty to the state.*

can find some way or method to make
my husband pay the price for these evils,
keep silent, for although a woman is
275    in other ways fearful and afraid to fight,
unable even to look at weapons,
when she finds herself wronged by her husband,
there is no heart more eager for blood.

Chorus
I will do it, for you punish your husband
280    justly, Medea, and I do not wonder
that you are pained by this misfortune.
But, I see Creon, lord of this land,
coming, to announce some new tidings.

[Enter Creon with guards from offstage.]

Creon
You, sullen and angry at your husband,
285    Medea, I declare that you must leave
this land in exile, taking your two children
with you, and don't delay at all. As I
am the enforcer of this decree,
I will not return home before I've tossed
290    you beyond the borders of my land.

Medea
Alas! I am woefully, utterly destroyed!
My enemies have opened my sails to the wind,
and there is no haven to escape ruin.
Still, though I have suffered badly, I will ask:
295    Why do you send me from this land, Creon?

Creon
I'm afraid of you—no need to mince words—
afraid you'll hurt my child irreparably.
I have many reasons to suspect this:
you are by nature clever and skilled in evil,
300    and you are tormented by the loss
of your husband's bed. Also, I've heard that

you are threatening to do something to
every party of the wedding – him who gave,
him who received, and her who was given.
305   So I'm on my guard before I suffer.
Better I incur your wrath now, lady,
than be soft and regret it later.


### Medea

Oh, oh!
This is not the first time, Creon; no, often
310   before, my reputation has done me harm.
No sensible man ought to have his children
taught to be exceedingly clever; for,
besides the other disadvantage, sloth,[21]
they will earn malicious ill-will.  When you
315   put something clever before stupid people,
you will seem useless and not really smart;
but when the city thinks you superior
to those who seem to have abstruse knowledge,
you will annoy them.  I myself share this fate,
320   for, since I am clever, some envy me,
others hate me; and I am not even
so very clever.  Do you, then, fear that
you will suffer something unpleasant from me?
This is unnecessary.  Do not worry,
325   Creon, that I would do harm to a king.
Furthermore, what wrong have you done to me?
You gave your daughter to the one your heart
chose for you.  Rather, it is my husband
whom I hate, but you, I think, acted sensibly.
330   I do not begrudge you that your affairs
turn out fairly.  Get married, and good luck
to you all!  Just let me dwell in this land;
for even though I am dishonored, I will
be silent, defeated by greater beings.


### Creon

335   Your words are soothing to hear; but in my heart
I fear that even now you are plotting
something wicked, and so I am even

[21]*a reference to the common Greek idea that education made men less vigorous*

less inclined to yield to you. A woman
with a hot temper, and even more so a man,
340    is easier to guard against than one
silent and clever.  Go as soon as you can;
do not argue, for these matters are fixed.
Not even you have the skill to remain
near us while you are hateful to me.

22A suppliant*
would often grasp
the knees of the
person being
beseeched.

[Medea bows before him and embraces his knees.22]

Medea
345    No, by your knees and newly married daughter!

Creon
You can stop arguing; you'll never persuade me.

Medea
You would expel me and dishonor my prayers?

Creon
Since I don't love you more than my own family.

Medea
350    O fatherland, now I hold only your memory!

Creon
Besides my children, I love my country most.

Medea
Oh, oh, love is such a great evil for mortals!

Creon
It goes as circumstances direct, I think.

Medea
Zeus, may he who deserves this pain not escape you!

Creon
355    Go, foolish woman, and save me the trouble.

*Medea*

> Trouble is what I have; I don't need more.

*Creon*

> You'll soon be pushed out by my guards' hands.

*Medea*

> Surely not that, I entreat you, Creon!

*Creon*

> You, it seems, will be a nuisance, lady.

*Medea*

360  We will leave; I have not begged you to gain this.

*Creon*

> Then why do you continue to press my hand?

*Medea*

> Suffer me to remain this one single day
> to consider where to make my exile
> and to plan for my boys, since their father
365  does not care enough to make an effort
> for his children. Pity them, for you also
> are a father and should be kind to them.
> I don't care about myself, but if we
> must go into exile, I lament
370  that they must endure this misfortune.

*Creon*

> I don't have a dictatorial nature,
> and I've often lost by being considerate—
> even now I see that I am making
375  a mistake, lady. Nevertheless,
> you shall have your request. But, mark my words,
> if the next sunrise sees you and your sons
> within the bounds of my kingdom, you will die.
> This is no idle threat. Now, if you must stay,
380  stay one day, for you will not do any
> of the terrible things I so fear.

*[Exit Creon with guards offstage.]*

Chorus
> Alas, alas,
> unfortunate in your troubles, poor woman,
> wherever will you turn to?  What friendship
385 or house or land will save you?
> Oh, God has carried you, Medea,
> into a pathless wave of troubles!

Medea
> It's turned out badly all around—who'd deny it?
> But not these things in this way—don't think that yet.
390 Those newlyweds still have struggles to come
> and those making the match no small labors.
> Do you think I would flatter that man
> if I had no plan or profit in it?
> I wouldn't even have spoken to him
395 or touched him with my hands, but he's become
> so foolish that, although he could have ruined
> my plans and cast me from this land, he allowed
> me to stay this day, in which I shall display
> the corpses of three of my enemies:
400 the father, the daughter, and my husband.
> Though there are many roads to death I might
> send them down, I don't yet know which I shall
>     choose,
> friends.  Will I set fire to the bridal house
405 or drive a sharp sword through their hearts, after
> I've sneaked through the house to where they sleep?
> There's just one little thing hindering me—
> if I am caught entering the house, scheming,
> I will die and become a source of laughter
410 for my enemies.  Better to take the straight road,
> in which I am so naturally skilled,
> and kill them with poison.
> So be it.
> And with them dead, what city will receive me?
415 What stranger will provide an asylum and
> a secure home and protect my person?

There is no one.  So, I'll stay here a bit longer.
If some safe tower shows itself to me,
then I'll pursue this murder by trick and stealth;
420     but if circumstance leaves me hanging here,
I'll take the sword myself, though it means death,
and kill them, and I'll go boldly into crime.
I swear by my mistress whom I worship
most of all and took as my ally long ago,
425     Hecate,[23] dwelling deep within my hearth,
none of them will hurt my heart and rejoice.
I will make these marriages bitter and
mournful for them, bitter my sorrow and
my exile from the land.  Come on, Medea,
430     spare nothing of what you know, planning and craft.
Go into the horror; it's a question
of endurance.  Do you see what you suffer?
You must not incur mockery through these
Corinthian marriages of Jason's,
435     you who are born from a good father and
from the Sun.[24] You know how to do this.
In addition, you were born a woman,
unable to do anything noble,
but so clever at everything evil.

Chorus[25]

Str. 1

440     The streams run up the holy rivers
       and justice and everything else is reversed:
Men have tricky counsels, and
       their faith does not stand firm in oaths,
whereas my reputation will turn and
445        have good fame.
Honor is coming to the race of women.
No more will ill-sounding fame hold women.

Ant. 1

The Muses will stop hymning my
       faithlessness in their old songs,
450     for Phoebus,[26] leader of songs, did not give
       to my comprehension the inspired song
of the lyre; since I would have sung a hymn

[23]*the goddess of witchcraft, associated with the moon and with crossroads; the domestic setting assigned to her by Medea is very unusual and indicates Medea's strangeness.*

[24]*Medea's paternal grandfather was the Sun god, Helios.*

[25]*In a stasimon, the Chorus reacts to all the events of the previous episode, usually in chronological order. Here, the Chorus first notes the unequal status of men and women, then deals with Medea's plan to murder the children.*

[26]*another name for Apollo, the god of music, poetry, and prophecy*

against the male race.
There is a great song with
455    much to say of my fate and that of men.

*Str. 2*

You sailed from the home of your fathers
        with a raging heart,
traveling through the twin rocks of Pontus,[27] and now
460            you live in a foreign land, having lost
the bed of your husbandless marriage,
poor woman, and dishonored you must
flee this land.

*Ant. 2*

The grace of oaths has gone; nor does shame
465        remain still in great Greece,
but has flown up to heaven. You have no father's
        house, unhappy woman, to shift your
anchorage towards, and another woman,
a princess, superior to your bed,
470        took over your house.

[Enter Jason from offstage.]

Jason[28]

This is not the first time that I've said it,
but harsh anger is an unbearable evil.[29]
You could have remained in this land and house,
if you had meekly obeyed the ruler's will;
475    but, because of rash words, you are thrown out
of the country. I have no problem with this;
keep on saying that Jason is the worst of men.
As for what you have said against the king,
think it a blessing that you are punished
480    only with exile. For my part, I always
tried to calm the king when he was angry;
I wanted you to stay; but you did not
let up your foolishness, always cursing
the king. Therefore, you are thrown out of this
485        country.
Still, after all this, I do not come here to fail
my friends, but to look after your lot, lady,

[27]*i.e. through the Black Sea*

[28]*The Greek audience would not need to be told who Jason was; they knew the story already, and his costume and mask indicated a hero in the prime of life.*

[29]*Characters often make general statements like this at the beginning of a speech.*

so that you and the children are not exiled
penniless or lacking anything.
490    Exile brings many evils with itself.
After all, even if you hate me,
I could never think badly of you.

*Medea*[30]
You entirely vile man—that's the greatest insult
my tongue can wield against your cowardice—
495    you come to us? You, the most hateful man alive?
This is neither boldness nor courage,
your looking friends in the face while hurting them,
but rather the greatest of all human
diseases: shamelessness. Still, you did well to come,
500    for I will speak and unburden my soul
in abusing you, and you will grieve to hear it.
I will start with the very beginning:
I saved you, as all the Greeks know who sailed
with you on your ship, the Argo.[31] You were
505    sent to master the fire-breathing bulls with yokes
and sow the deadly field. And the dragon
who was guarding the Golden Fleece, wrapped around it
with all those coils in eternal vigilance—
I killed it and gave you the light of salvation.
510    After betraying my father and my home,
I came to Iolcus with you, more eager than wise.
I killed Pelias in the worst way
for a man to die—by his own children's hands,
and I destroyed his whole house. You got
515    all this from me, you worst of men, and then
you betrayed me and got yourself a new bed,
even though you already had children.
If you were still childless, it would at least
be understandable for you to leave my bed.
520    The faith of oaths is over and gone—I wonder,
do you think that the gods of that time are
no longer in power, or that now men
have some new rules for what is just? Because
you know that you are not being faithful to me.
525    Oh, this right hand, which you touched often,

[30]*Greek tragedians, especially Euripides, often include an agon,\* or contest of speeches.*

[31]*Note how Euripides plays down Medea's supernatural powers as a witch.*

32Here Medea
clearly indicates
that she views
herself as Jason's
equal, not a typi-
cally submissive
woman. In fact,
she claims power
over Jason by
mentioning his
supplication of
her.

and these knees—how uselessly I was touched
by this bad man, and how I was mistaken!32
Come, I'll share with you as if you were my friend.
(Thinking to get something good from you?
530  No, but being questioned, you'll be proven base.)
Now where do I turn?  To my homeland and
my father's house, which I betrayed for you?
Or to those poor daughters of Pelias?
Wouldn't they receive me nicely in the house
535  where I killed their father? Because that's how it
        stands!
I've made myself hateful to my friends at home,
whom I would never hurt for my own sake;
but for you I hold them as enemies.
540  Accordingly, in return for these things,
you've made me blessed among Greek women:
I have you as my wonderful, faithful husband—
poor me!  I will go into exile from this,
bereft of friends, alone with only my children.
545  A pretty disgrace for a new bridegroom:
beggar children banished with me who saved you!
O Zeus, why did you grant men clear signs to tell
the purity of gold, when no stamp appears
on the body of men by which one can
550  know the good man from the evil-doer?33

33a common lament
in Euripidean
plays

Chorus

Anger is terrible and hard to heal,
when friends engage in strife against friends.

Jason

It seems I must argue that I'm not a bad man,
and, like the wise pilot of a ship, run out
555  from under the storm of your tongue-lashing
with only the tips of the sails, my lady.
Although you exalt yourself exceedingly,
I know that alone of gods and men
Aphrodite34 was the savior of my sailing.

34the goddess of
love and sexual
attraction

560  It's true you have a subtle mind, but it
would be in poor taste to tell how Love with his

unavoidable arrows made you save my skin.[35]
I'll not put matters so precisely.
565    Of course, you didn't do badly when you
       helped me. In fact, you took greater than you gave
       from my salvation, as I shall explain.
       First of all, you live in Greece instead of
       a barbarian land, and you know justice
570    and how to use laws instead of force.[36]
       All the Greeks know that you are clever,
       and you are famous; but if you lived at
       the ends of the earth, there'd be no account of you.
       For me I'd rather not have gold at home,
575    nor would I sing sweeter than Orpheus,[37]
       if no one would know about me.[38] I've said
       so much to you about my adventures,
       since you started this competition of words.
       As for your reproaches against my royal
580    marriage, first I'll show you that I was wise
       in this matter, and, second, restrained; and
       third, a great friend to you and my children.
       Keep quiet!
       When I arrived here from Iolcus, besieged
585    by many impossible disasters,
       what luckier windfall could I find than this:
       though an exile, to marry the king's daughter?
       It's not what worries you so much—that I hate
       your bed and am struck by desire of a new bride,
590    or am making an effort to outdo the number
       of your children. Those who are born are enough;
       I don't hate them. But how—and this is the
       biggest thing—could we live happily and not
       in poverty, knowing that every friend
595    he meets flees a poor man, when I could raise
       children in a way worthy of my house,
       beget brothers to those children from you
       and join the houses together and be happy?
       What need of children do you have? As for me,
600    there's profit in helping the living children
       with those to come. Surely I've not reasoned badly?
       You wouldn't say so, if your empty bed

[35]*In Greek mythology, Eros (Love), son of Aphrodite, is portrayed as a boy with a golden bow who shoots arrows of desire at unlucky victims. Not even Zeus can resist these arrows.*

[36]*Most of the Greek audience of the play would agree with these sentiments, even though Jason is an unsympathetic character.*

[37]*the most famous singer of mythology, who could charm animals and even Death with his songs*

[38]*The idea that a life of suffering, yet one that leads to fame, is better than a long happy life without glory is a theme of many Greek heroes.*

didn't annoy you.  It's gotten so you
women think you have everything when
605     it's good in your bedroom, but if some misfortune
strikes your chamber, you think even the best
and fairest things are the most adverse.
It would be better if men could get children
some other way, and there were no female race.
610     That way there would be no trouble for men.[39]

[39]An even more
extreme version of
this wish is voiced
by the title char-
acter in Euripides'
Hippolytus.

Chorus
Jason, you arranged your words well, but, still,
to me, if I may speak frankly, I think
that you've unjustly betrayed your wife.

Medea
Well, I'm different from many people
615     in that I think whoever is unjust,
but clever at speaking deserves the greatest
punishment of all.  When someone is overbold
in sugar-coating injustice with his tongue,
there's nothing he won't dare.  Still, he's not so smart.
620     The same with you:  to me now you don't seem suave
or clever at speaking—one word will catch you.
If you really weren't ashamed, you should have
persuaded me and then gotten married,
but you kept quiet about this to your friends.

Jason
625     You would have been very supportive indeed,
if I'd told you about the marriage, when
even now you can't check the bile from your heart.

Medea
That wasn't your concern, but rather how
proper old men don't have barbarian wives.

Jason
630     Know this well: it was not for a wife
that I made this royal marriage; but,
just as I said before, wishing to save

you and to sow princes of the same blood
as my children, a safeguard for the house.

*Medea*

635    May I never have a happy life that
gives me pain, or wealth that annoys my mind!

*Jason*

You could change your prayer and seem wiser:
Pray never to say that good things give you pain
and not to seem unhappy when you're doing well.

*Medea*

640    You insult me, because you have an escape
route, while I will flee this land alone.

*Jason*

You chose this course; don't blame anyone else.

*Medea*

What did I do? Get married and betray you?

*Jason*

You cursed the royal house with unholy words.

*Medea*

645    And in your house, too, I am accursed.

*Jason*

Well, I won't debate this matter further with you.
Rather, if you want to take some of my money
for the children or yourself, to help you
in your exile, tell me, as I'm ready
650    to give with an ungrudging hand and to send
a token to my foreign friends, so they'll help you.
Don't be willfully foolish in this, too, lady,
but let your anger go and reap the reward.

*Medea*

We wouldn't make use of your foreign friends

655        or accept anything; don't give to us,
           for the gifts of a wicked man are no help.

Jason
           Then I call the gods to witness how I
           would do anything to help you and the children,
660        but good things don't please you.  You just stubbornly
           push your friends away.  And so you'll suffer more.

                                        [Exit Jason offstage.]

Chorus
                                                              Str. 1

           Excessive Love gives men
           neither glory nor virtue,
           but if Aphrodite comes in moderation,
665             no other god is so gracious.
           Mistress, may you never release at me
                an irresistible arrow
           anointed with desire from your golden bow.

                                                              Ant. 1

           Moderation nurtures me,
670        the fairest gift of the gods.
           May terrible Aphrodite never strike me
                with disputed anger and insatiate strife
           and send my heart towards other beds,
                but revere harmonious marriages
675        and intelligently decide where women sleep.

                                                              Str. 2

           O fatherland, O home, never let me be
                without my city,
           leading a life of impossibility, difficult
                to endure, the most pitiful of pains.
680        Let me die, let me die instead,
           finishing my day of life!
           No other hardship exceeds
           losing one's native land.

                                                              Ant. 2

           We saw it ourselves, I can tell the story
685             not learned from others.

No city, no friend pities you who have
    suffered the most terrible of sufferings.
May he perish without grace
whoever does not open a clean mind
690   and honor his friends.
He certainly will never be a friend of mine.

*[Enter Aegeus from offstage.]*

*Aegeus*
   Hello, Medea! No one knows a better
   salutation to greet friends than this!

*Medea*
   Hello to you, too, son of wise Pandion,
695   Aegeus. What brings you to this part of earth?

*Aegeus*
   I've just left Apollo's ancient oracle.

*Medea*
   Why did you seek the prophetic world-navel?[40]

*Aegeus*
   I asked how children might be born to me.

*Medea*
   By the gods, you are still childless at your age?

*Aegeus*
700   By some divine will I still have no children.

*Medea*
   Do you have a wife, or is your bed empty?

*Aegeus*
   I do not lack a nuptial couch.

*Medea*
   What did Phoebus say to you about children?

[40]*Delphi was called this because it marked the center of the earth, which the Greeks considered a point of contact between the human world and the gods' territory.*

[41] The oracles from Delphi were in verse and often came in the form of riddles.

[42] It was sometimes forbidden to reveal an oracle to others.

[43] This oracle's riddle is actually quite easy to solve. Apollo has promised that Aegeus will conceive a child the next time he has intercourse, so he must not sleep with any other woman before his wife.

[44] In some stories, Pittheus* tricked Aegeus into sleeping with his daughter, so this comment could be quite ironic.

Aegeus

Words wiser than a man can understand.[41]

Medea

705    Is it right for me to know the god's reply?[42]

Aegeus

Certainly, for it requires a wise mind.

Medea

What did he say?  Tell me, if I may listen.

Aegeus

That I not loosen the wineskin's protruding foot.

Medea

Before doing something or arriving somewhere?

Aegeus

710    Before I arrive at my ancestral hearth.[43]

Medea

Then why are you making a sea journey by land?

Aegeus

A man called Pittheus, lord of Troezen.

Medea

Son of Pelops, they say, a very pious man.

Aegeus

I want to share the god's response with him.

Medea

715    He's a wise man and skilled in such matters.

Aegeus

And dearest to me of all my close friends.[44]

Medea

Then good luck and may you find all you desire.

*Aegeus*
> But why is your face so pale and sad?

*Medea*
> Aegeus, my husband is the worst of men.

*Aegeus*
720   What's this?  Tell me clearly of your trouble.

*Medea*
> Jason injures me, though he's suffered nothing.

*Aegeus*
> What did he do?  Tell me more clearly.

*Medea*
> He has taken a wife in my place.

*Aegeus*
> Has he really dared this most shameful deed?

*Medea*
725   You know it.  We, his old friends, are dishonored.

*Aegeus*
> Was he in love, or did he hate your bed?

*Medea*
> Deeply in love.  He wasn't born faithful to friends.

*Aegeus*
> Well, if this is true, he is a bad man.

*Medea*
> Deeply in love with a tie to the royal house.

*Aegeus*
730   Who gave him the bride?  Finish the story for me.

*Medea*
> Creon, who rules this land of Corinth.

*Aegeus*

I can certainly see why you are grieved, lady.

*Medea*

I'm done for—I'm also being banished from the land.

*Aegeus*

By whom?  Tell me of this new problem.

*Medea*

735    Creon drives me as an exile from Corinth.

*Aegeus*

Jason allows it?  I don't approve of that!

*Medea*

Not in word, but he's eager to endure it.
Please, I beseech you by your beard and your knees!
I am your suppliant.  Pity me,
pity this poor woman!  Don't watch me go
740    into exile alone, but accept me
as a guest into your land and home.
Thus may the gods grant your desire with children,
and may you die blessed!  You don't know the windfall
you've found.  I will stop your childlessness and make
745    you able to beget sons; I know the right drugs.[45]

*Aegeus*

I am eager to grant you this grace for
many reasons—first, because of the gods;
second, because of the children whose births
you announce, for in this I am entirely lost.
750    This is how it is with me: When you come
to my land, I will try to help you with
justice on my side.  You yourself must find
a way from this land; but if you come to my house,
you will stay safely and I will surrender
755    you to no one, though I wish to be
blameless to my foreign friends as well.

[45]Medea also understands the oracle, but is manipulating Aegeus.

*Medea*

So be it!  But, if I had a pledge of these things
from you, I would be satisfied with your end.

*Aegeus*

Don't you trust me?  Or is something bothering you?

*Medea*

760    I do, but the house of Pelias is
       hostile to me, and Creon, too. If you
       are bound by oath, you won't give me up
       when they come for me; but if we go only
       by words, and not oaths to the gods, you might
       be their friend and heed their demands, perhaps,
765    for I am weak, while they have wealth and power.

*Aegeus*

You have shown much forethought with your words;
if you think it best, I won't refuse it.
It is safer for me also to have
some excuse to give your enemies,
770    and you'll be surer of yourself. Choose the gods.

*Medea*

Swear by the Earth and the Sun,[46] father of
my father, and the whole race of gods together.[47]

*Aegeus*

To do what?  Or not to do something?  Tell me.

*Medea*

That you will never expel me from your land,
775    and, if one of my enemies comes for me,
       that you'll not give me up willingly while you live.

*Aegeus*

I swear by the Earth and the bright light of the Sun
and all the gods to abide by what you've said.

[46]The Sun was
often invoked
because he was
thought to witness
all human activ-
ity; the connection
to Medea is coin-
cidental.

[47]a typical group-
ing of gods for an
oath; the grouping
of all the gods
together was done
so that no perti-
nent deity would
be accidentally
left out.

48Greek oaths usually included a clause for punishment if the oath was broken.

49The audience would know that Medea was later forced to flee Athens when she tried to secretly kill Aegeus' son Theseus, so there is some irony in this scene.

50the messenger god and patron of travellers

*Medea*
Good.  What will you suffer if you break the oath?[48]

*Aegeus*
780     That which comes to impious mortals.

*Medea*
Then go on your way rejoicing, for all is well!
I'll come to your city as soon as I can,
when I've taken care of my affairs here.[49]

[Exit Aegeus offstage.]

*Chorus*
May Lord Hermes[50] walk with you
785     as your guide home, and may you accomplish
that which you eagerly work for, since
you are a noble man, Aegeus,
in my opinion.

*Medea*
By Zeus and divine Justice and light of the Sun,
790     now, friends, I have glorious victory
over my enemies, my foot is on the road!
Now I know my enemies will pay the price.
This man is like a harbor for the plans
I've been striving towards. I can tack my sails
795     on him and steer for the city and
bastion of Athena.  Now I shall tell you
all my plans, no leisurely conversation.
I will send one of my servants to ask
Jason to come and see me.  When he comes,
800     I will speak soothing words to him, how I think
he's right, he made a good marriage with the king—
the marriage he has now that he's betrayed us—
that it's prudent, he knew what he was doing.
But I'll ask that my sons be allowed to stay—
805     not that I would leave them in a hostile land,
but so that I can trick and kill the princess.
I shall send them bearing gifts to her,

a delicate dress and golden crown.
When she takes them and puts them on her skin,
810    she will die horribly—and so will
anyone who touches her! I will
anoint the gifts with powerful poisons.
Now, however, I dismiss the subject.
I mourn the deed that I must do then,
815    for I will kill my own children. There is
no one who will save them; and when I have
obliterated the whole house of Jason,
I will leave the land, fleeing the murder
of my dearest children, having dared the most
820    unholy deed, for I will not suffer
my enemies to mock me, my friends.
It was a mistake to leave my father's house,
trusting the words of a Greek man, who,
with God's help, will pay the penalty to me.
825    He'll never see the children born from me
grow up, nor will he sire a child from his
newly-yoked bride, since she must die a horrible
death from my poisons. Let no one think me
weak or helpless or calm, but the other sort,
830    hard on enemies and kind to friends.[51]
People like this live the most famous lives.

*Chorus*
Since you shared your plan with us, I want to
help you and aid the laws of humanity:
please don't do this.

*Medea*
835    It cannot be otherwise. I understand
why you speak this way—you've not suffered like me.

*Chorus*
Do you dare to kill your children, woman?

*Medea*
Because it will hurt my husband most of all.

[51]*This was the Greek idea of virtue and heroic behavior from Homeric times into the Christian period.*

Chorus

But you would become the most wretched of women!

Medea

840        So be it.  Everything else is details.

*[to one of her attendants[52]]*

Go and fetch Jason.  I use you in all
my confidential affairs.  Please say nothing
of my decisions, if you think well
of your mistress and were born a woman.

*[Exit attendant offstage.]*

*[52]She speaks to a mute\* character not otherwise mentioned in the manuscript.*

*[53]i.e. the Athenians, whose first king was Erechtheus*

Chorus

                                                                    *Str. 1*

845        The children of Erechtheus[53] have long been happy,
children of the blessed gods, from
a holy, unconquered land, enjoying
the most famous wisdom, always walking
luxuriously through the clearest air, where
850        once, they say, the nine holy Muses of Pieria
gave birth to golden Harmony;

                                                                    *Ant. 1*

where, they boast, Aphrodite draws water
from the beautiful-flowing streams of Cephisus
and breathes down over the land
855        measured, sweet-smelling breezes, and her hair
is crowned with a fragrant garland of flowers
by the Cupids, companions of Wisdom,
helpers in every kind of excellence.

                                                                    *Str. 2*

How, therefore, will this city
860        of holy rivers, this land
that receives and helps its friends,
accept you, the child murderer,
unholy in the sight of others?
Consider the blow against your children!
865        Consider the murder you undertake!
Don't—we are, all of us, all
together, suppliants at your knees—
                don't kill your children!

Where will you take the courage of heart
870 and hand to pursue this terrible daring
against the children?
How will you keep the tears
from your eyes when you look at them,
how will you keep your resolve
875 to kill them?  You won't be able,
when your sons fall down and plead,
to soak your hand in their blood
        with your daring heart.

*[Enter Jason with attendants.]*

Jason

I am here as requested.  Even though
880 you are angry, you won't lack this: I'll listen.
What new thing do you want from me, lady?

Medea

Jason, I ask you to forgive what I said
before; it is logical for you to bear
my anger, since we two have done many acts
885 of kindness for each other in the past.
I had a conversation with myself
and scolded myself, "Madwoman, why do I rave
and hate those wishing to help me?  Why do I
make myself an enemy to the rulers
890 of this land and my husband, who is doing
everything to help us, marrying
the princess and siring brothers to my children?
Why don't I stop being angry?  Why do
I suffer, when the gods are treating me well?
895 Don't I have children?  And don't I know
that we are exiled and lacking friends?"
After these thoughts I perceived that I've been
very foolish and overly emotional.
Now, therefore, I applaud you and think you quite
900        restrained
to take up my problem when I was foolish,
who ought to have embraced these plans

54*These lines imag-
ine Medea playing
the role of the
bride's mother in a
traditional Greek
wedding.*

and helped see them through, standing by your bed
and taking delight in caring for your bride.[54]
905     But, we are what we are—I won't say wicked,
just women, so you must not conform to
my bad conduct, nor answer foolish words
with foolish words.  I seek pardon and agree that
I spoke badly then, but I've rethought it all now.
910     O children, children, come here, leave the house.

*[The Children and Tutor enter from the house.]*
Come out—embrace and greet your father with me,
and with Mother end our feud with a friend.
We have made peace, all the anger is gone!
Take his right hand—oh!  I'm thinking of evils
915     hidden in the future.  O children, will you,
after living a long life, stretch out your
loving arms to me like that when I'm dead?
Poor me, how close to tears I am and full of fear!
After ending this long quarrel with your
920     father, my tender eyes have filled with tears.

## Chorus

My eyes also are taken by wet tears;
may this evil not grow greater than it is now!

## Jason

My lady, I applaud your new words and
do not blame the earlier ones!  It is
925     natural for the female race to be angry
at a husband when he smuggles in a new wife.
But, your heart has changed for the better,
and you learned, albeit with time, that you were
defeated—that's the sign of a prudent woman.
930     For you, boys, your father has not unwisely
gained great security, with God's help,
for I think you'll be the first men of
Corinth together with your brothers.
Just grow up; everything else your father
935     has achieved—and whichever god loves him.
I want to see you solidly built when you

reach the end of youth, stronger than my enemies.
You there, why are your eyes wet with tears?
Why have you turned your white cheek away?
940    Did I say something to displease you?

*Medea*

It's nothing.  I was thinking about these children.

*Jason*

Cheer up!  I will see it turns out well for them.

*Medea*

I will do as you say; certainly I
will not reproach your words, but women are
945    naturally delicate and close to tears.

*Jason*

Why do you moan so much over the children?

*Medea*

I bore them:  when you prayed for them to live,
worry came to me that it might not happen.
But, you came here to discuss certain matters—
950    some I've said, but I will now relate the rest.
Since the king banishes me (to me, also,
this is a good idea: I know now
I should not be in your way, nor dwell in
the king's land, since I seem hostile to their house),
955    I, then, will depart this land in exile, but
for the children, ask Creon to let them stay,
so that they may grow up under your care.

*Jason*

I don't know if I can sway him, but I'll try.

*Medea*

Then ask your wife to entreat her father
960    not to expel the children from the country.

Jason
    Yes, certainly, and I think I'll persuade her,
    if she is like other women, anyway.

Medea
    I will help you in this task, for I will
    send her gifts far fairer than any
965    in existence now, I know it, a fine dress
    and a golden crown that the children will bear.

*[to her attendants]*
    One of you, quickly, fetch here the costume.
    She will be happy not in one way only,
    but ten thousand, finding a peerless husband
970    like you for her bed and acquiring a costume
    that the Sun, my grandfather, once gave to his
    offspring. Take it for her dowry, boys,
    in your hands, and give it to the princess,
    the blessed bride; she will not despise these gifts.

Jason
975    Why, silly woman, are you emptying your hands
    of these things? Do you think the royal house
    lacks dresses? Or gold? Keep them, don't give them
        away.
    If my wife thinks anything of me, she will
    put my words before money, I'm sure of it.

Medea
980    Don't be like this with me. Gifts persuade even
    the gods, as the saying goes; for mortals,
    gold is better than ten thousand words.
    God watches over her, God increases
    her power. As a young woman she already
985    rules; but I would give up my life to save
    my sons from exile, not only my gold.
    Now, children, go into the wealthy house
    and supplicate your father's new wife,
    my mistress; when you give her the costume,
990    ask not to be exiled. It is crucial

that she take the gifts with her own hand.
Go as quick as you can, and then be the
messengers of good news to your mother
when you come back to tell her that you have
995    made all her wishes come true.

> *[Exit Jason with the Children, Tutor, and his*
> *attendants offstage.]*

*Chorus*

*Str. 1*

Now my hope is gone that the boys will live,
    gone—for they are already going into death.
The bride will accept the golden headband;
poor thing, she will accept her ruin.
1000    She will put around her golden hair
      the costume of Death—
      she with her own hands.

*Ant. 1*

The charm will persuade her, and the
    heavenly gleam to put on
1005    the dress and the crown wrought of gold.
She'll wear her bridal garb among the dead.
Thus she'll be lured into the net,
    poor thing, into her fate.
    She will not escape her ruin.

*Str. 2*

1010    And you, wretched man, disastrously
    married to royal kin,
unknowingly, you are bringing
mortal destruction to your sons and
    hateful death to your wife.
1015    Poor man, how much you misunderstand your destiny.

*Ant. 2*

And I groan with your pains, O
    wretched mother of these boys,
who will murder her children
because of a bridal bed that your husband
1020    left behind along with you
unlawfully to live with another consort.

*[Enter the Tutor with the Children from offstage.]*

**Tutor**
> Mistress, the children are released from exile,
> and the princess bride gladly took the gifts into
> her hands.  The palace sees the children in peace.

1025 > Hey—
> why are you troubled when things are going well?

**Medea**
> Alas!

**Tutor**
> I don't understand your reaction to this news.

**Medea**
> Again, alas!

**Tutor**
>                        I certainly don't know

1030 > what misfortune is in these tidings; am
> I mistaken by their pleasant appearance?

**Medea**
> You announced what you announced. I don't blame
>          you.

**Tutor**
> Why do you lower your eyes and weep?

**Medea**

1035 > I have reason to do so, old man, for the gods—
> and I in my madness—have devised these things.

**Tutor**
> Cheer up!  You'll return soon, through your sons'
>          influence.

**Medea**
> I'll bring back others before this poor woman.[55]

[55]*an ironic joke; it would be more likely for Medea's influence to allow the return of other exiles than for her to ever be allowed back in Corinth.*

*Tutor*

1040　You're not the first woman to be separated
　　　from her children. To bear misfortune lightly
　　　is the duty of every mortal.

*Medea*

　　　I will, but you, go inside the house and
　　　prepare what the children need for the day.

　　　　　　　　　　　*[Exit Tutor into the house.]*

1045　[56]O children, children, this is your city
　　　and home, where, after you have left poor me,
　　　you will dwell, forever without your mother.
　　　I am exiled to another land,
　　　before I could enjoy you or see you happy,
1050　before I could decorate your brides'
　　　chamber and lift high the wedding torch.
　　　Oh, a wretched woman for my boldness!
　　　In vain, children, did I give you birth,
　　　in vain I suffered and was torn by labors,
1055　　，
　　　an enviable thing for men.  Now, that
　　　sweet thought is destroyed, for, bereft of you,
　　　I will always lead a sad and painful life.
　　　You will no longer see your mother with your
1060　dear eyes, heading into another type of life.
　　　Oh, oh—why do you look at me with those eyes,
　　　children?[57] Why do you smile this final smile?
　　　Alas!  What will I do?  My heart is gone,
　　　ladies, seeing the beaming eye of my sons.
1065　I could not—enough of those former plans!
　　　I will take my children out of the country.
　　　Why must I hurt their father with evils
　　　that will hurt me twice as badly?  I won't!
　　　Enough of those plans!
1070　Although, why should I suffer?  Will I
　　　endure the mockery of my enemies
　　　when I've let them get off unpunished?
　　　It must be dared.  This is just weakness,
　　　to keep admitting soft words to my mind.

[56]*one of the most famous speeches in Greek tragedy; Medea's psychological agony as she debates with herself is expressed with supreme rhetorical skill and poetic beauty.*

[57]*It is not necessary to ask what the children might think when they hear their mother's speech, because children were not considered capable of rational thought; they were almost props.*

1075    Go inside, children. To anyone who is
        not allowed to be present at my sacrifice,
        that is your concern![58] I will not hold back my hand!
        Ah, ah!
        Don't do it, heart, don't do these things yourself.

1080    Let them go, poor woman, spare the children.
        Living there with you they will make you happy.
        No, by the avenging demons of Hell,
        it can never be that I provide a way
        for my enemies to mistreat my children.

1085    It's already been done; there is no escape.
        The crown is surely on her head, and the
        princess bride is dying in the dress, I know.
        But, since I am going down the most daring road
        and will send them down one still more daring,

1090    I wish to look at my sons. Children, give
        your right hand to your mother to caress!
        O dearest hands! and dearest mouths and shape
        and beautiful face of my children!
        May you be happy…just there. Your father has

1095    taken it all here. O honey-sweet embrace,
        O softest skin and most delightful breath of my sons!
        Go, go! I can no longer look at you,
        but am overcome by weakness. I am
        learning what evils I am about to commit,

1100    but my heart is greater than my mind,
        the cause of the greatest griefs for mortals.[59]

                            [Exit the Children into the house.]

Chorus[60]
        Often before now, I have pondered
        thought more subtle, and I have gone
        into debates greater than the race of

1105    women ought to examine.
        But, we also have a muse, who teaches
        us to make us wise, not all of us,
        but a small group (you might find one
        among many) of women are

[58] *a darkly humorous allusion to the language of Greek sacrifice*

[59] *These last lines were particularly resonant with Greek and Roman philosophy, which saw this speech and Medea in general as symbolic of the eternal human struggle between reason and emotion.*

[60] *an unusual anapestic interlude instead of the expected lyric*

1110    uninspired.
        And I say that of mortals, those
        who have no experience at all
        with children are luckier than those
        who have them.
1115    Childless people, who never learn
        whether children are a blessing
        or a pain, avoid many
        troubles.
        Parents with sweet children at home,
1120    I see their time used up in care:
        how to nurture them well and
        give them a good livelihood;
        and whether they are laboring
        for noble men or wicked
1125    is unclear.
        One thing I denounce as the worst
        evil of all for humanity:
        even after you've found means enough
        and the children grow into youth
1130    and become noble, if God wills,
        Death goes off to Hades carrying
        the bodies of your children.
        How, then, is it worthwhile
        if, in addition to the other
1135    labors for the sake of children,
        God adds this most heartrending pain?

Medea
        My friends, I've been standing here all this time
        eagerly awaiting the news from the palace.
        And indeed, I see this man, one of Jason's
1140    attendants, approaching.  His strained breath
        shows that he will announce some new evil.

*[Enter Messenger from offstage.]*

Messenger
        Medea, flee, flee!  Neglect passage
        neither by land nor by sea, by ship or road.

1145  *Medea*

What has happened that I must fly like this?

*Messenger*

The young princess has just perished, and Creon
her father, at the hands of your poisons.

*Medea*

A most beautiful tale you've told, and I will count
you as a friend and benefactor forever!

1150  *Messenger*

What?  Do you understand rightly, or are you
mad, my lady?  You've outrageously damaged
the royal hearth, and you're happy, unafraid?

*Medea*

I could reply to these words of yours,
but don't be hasty, my friend; just tell me:
how did they die?  You will delight me
1155      twice as much, if they died really terribly.

*Messenger*

When your sons came with their father and entered
the bridal house, we slaves who were distressed
by your troubles were delighted; quickly
the gossip passed through our ears that you and
1160      your husband had ceased your previous quarrel.
One slave kissed the children's hands, while another
tousled their blond heads.  I myself with happiness
followed the boys to the women's quarters.
The mistress whom we honor now instead of you,
1165      before she saw the pair of your children,
cast an eager eye at Jason; then,
however, she cast down her eyes and turned
away her white cheek, in disgust at
the children's entrance.  But your husband
1170      took away the young lady's anger and bile,
saying, "Please don't be bitter towards friends,

but cease being proud and turn back your head,
recognizing your husband's friends as your own,
and accept these gifts and ask your father
1175 to release these children from exile,
as a favor to me." When she saw the costume,
she did not hold back, but granted it all
to her man, and before the father and
your sons had gone far from the house, she took
1180 the colorful dress and put it on;
placing the golden crown around her curls,
she arranged her hair with a shining mirror,
smiling at the lifeless image of her body.
Then she rose from her chair and left the room,
1185 walking luxuriously with her white foot,
over-exulting in the gifts, and many,
many times stretching back her leg to better
admire her gown. Then, however, it was
a terrible sight to behold, for,
1190 her complexion altered, she went back slantwise,
her limbs shaking, and she almost fell
onto the chair to avoid hitting the ground.
Some old woman, a servant, thinking, I suppose,
that she was possessed by Pan or some other god,[61]
1195 shouted, "Eleleu!"[62] before she could see
white foam coming from her mouth and the girl's eyes
twisting in their sockets, the blood gone from her face.
Then instead of singing hallelujah
came a great shriek. One maid rushed off at once
1200 into the father's house, and the maid
to the new husband, to tell him of his bride's
misfortune. The whole house was quaking with
heavy running. A fast sprinter would
already have reached the tape—that's how fast
1205 the princess moved—breaking her silence and
opening her eyes to groan terribly,
for a second pain had attacked her:
The golden crown lying on her head sent
out a stream of all-devouring fire,
1210 and the fine dress, gifts of your children,
devoured the ill-starred girl's white flesh.

ode.[61]*Spiritual ecstasy* * *of this kind was an accepted part of Greek religion.*

[62]*the usual cry of religious ecstasy*

She stood up from the chair and fled, burning,
trying to tear off the crown; but the gold
chain held her tightly in its clutch, and the fire,
1215 when she shook her head, burned twice as brightly.
Defeated by her suffering, she fell
to the ground, difficult to recognize
except by a parent, for the form of her eyes
was not clear, nor her beautiful face,
1220 and blood was dripping from the top of her head,
burning with fire, her flesh flowing off the bone
like pine sap from the poison's hidden teeth,
a terrible sight. Everyone was
afraid to touch the corpse, for we had
1225 her misfortune as our teacher. Her father,
however—poor man, in ignorance
of the disaster, he came suddenly
into the house and fell on the corpse.
He groaned and embraced her, kissing her hands,
1230 crying, "My poor child, what god has destroyed
you so pitifully? Who makes this old man,
one foot in the grave, bereft of you?
Oh, would that I could die with you, child!"
When he stopped wailing and groaning, the old man
1235 tried to stand up, but the fine dress, like ivy
on the branches of a laurel, clung to his skin,
the struggling was terrible. The more he tried
to rise to his knees, the more she held on.
If he used force, he was just tearing the flesh
1240 off his own old bones. In time he gave up
and, unfortunate man, let go his soul,
for he could no longer fight the evil,
The corpses lay there, the young girl with her
old father close by, a disaster regretted
1245 with tears. Your side of it I will leave out
of the story, for yourself will know the return
of punishment. Humanity is, I think—
and not for the first time now—a shadow,
nor would I hesitate to say that those
1250 who seem wise and are anxious about words,
those men pay the greatest penalty for
stupidity. No human being is

a happy man; when wealth is flowing towards him,
he might be luckier than another man,
1255 but not truly happy. [63]

*[Exit Messenger offstage.]*

Chorus
God seems to have cast many evils at
Jason on this day—justly. How we pity
your misfortune, poor daughter of Creon,
dying for your marriage to Jason.
1260

*Medea*
Friends, I have decided to kill my sons
and set out from this land as soon as possible,
and not to allow with my delay some
more hostile hand to slay my children.
It is absolutely necessary
1265 for them to die, but since it must be,
then I who gave them life will take it.
But, arm yourself for this, heart. Why do I
delay these terrible, evil necessities?
Come, wretched hand of mine, take the sword.
1270 Take it, and head for the sad starting block
of the rest of your life. Don't be a coward,
don't remember your children as your dearest ones,
how you bore them, but for this one short day,
forget your sons. Mourn them later. Even
1275 if you kill them, still, they are dear. I am
an unlucky woman.

*[Exit Medea into the house.]*

Chorus
Str. 1

O Earth and brilliant
    ray of the Sun, look down, look at this
    lost woman, before she puts her
1280    bloody, murderous hand to her children.
For she is sprung from your golden
    seed, and it is fearful for the blood

[63]*These lines express one of the most important ideas of the Greek worldview, which can be paraphrased, "Call no man happy until he is dead."*

of a god to be spilled by men.
But, O heaven-born light, hinder her,
1285          stop her, take from this home that
poor, murderous Fury, driven by revenge.

*Ant. 1*

In vain the labor of children is lost,
1290          in vain, indeed, you bore that dear race,
O you who left the dark-blue rock of the
Symplegades, that most inhospitable passage.
Wretched woman, why does heart-oppressing wrath
fall on you, and why does terrible
murder answer murder?
1295          Pollution from relatives is difficult for mortals,
and it brings grief to kinslayers in tune with
their crime, falling on their house by god's will.

*Child*
1300          *[from within the house]*
Oh, no!

*Chorus*

*Str. 2*

Do you hear the cry?  Do you hear the child?
Oh, poor thing, O unlucky woman!

*First Child*
What do I do?  Where can I escape Mother's hands?

*Second Child*
I don't know, dearest brother; we're done for!

*Chorus*
1305          Should I go into the house?  I think I should stop
the murder for the children.

*First Child*
Yes, by the gods, stop it!  The time is critical![64]
*Second Child*
We are almost in the clutches of her sword!

[64]The response
by someone in
the house to the
Chorus is unusual
for Greek tragedy.

Chorus[65]
>Wretched woman, truly you were always made
>>of stone or iron, if you can kill
>>with murderous fate
1310
>>>the children that you bore.

*Ant. 2*

>One other, I've heard of one other woman of
>>all before us who attacked her dear children.[66]
>Ino, driven mad by the gods, when the wife
>>of Zeus sent her wandering from her home.
1315
>She fell, poor woman, into the sea, in an
>>impious murder of her children,
>>stepping too far on the promontory,
>>and she perished, dying with her two sons.
>After this, is anything too horrible to happen?
1320
>>O bed of women, site of many labors,
>>how many evils you have already
>>brought to humanity.

*[Enter Jason with attendants from offstage.]*
1325

Jason
>Ladies who stand by this house, is the one
>who has created this horror, Medea—
>is she at home or already fled?
>Truly, she must either hide under the earth
>or lift her body on wings into the sky
>if she does not wish to pay the penalty
>to the king's house. Does she believe that
1330
>after she's killed this land's royalty
>she will escape this house without punishment?
>Really, though, I care not so much for her
>as for the children. Those whom she has harmed
>will harm her, but I came to save the lives
>of my sons, lest the family do something
1335
>to them I will regret in vengeance
>for their mother's unholy murder.

Chorus
>Poor man, you don't know the evil you've come into,
>Jason, or you would not have said those words.

[65]Note how quickly the Chorus gives up the idea of interfering. They are bystanders, not part of the action.

[66]A strange statement, as Greek mythology contains many examples of women killing their children, often in acts of revenge against their husbands.

1340  *Jason*

　　　　Why?  Or does she want to kill me, too?

　　　　*Chorus*

　　　　Your children have died at their mother's hands.

　　　　*Jason*

　　　　What do you mean?  You've destroyed me, lady!

　　　　*Chorus*

　　　　I mean you shouldn't think your children still live.

　　　　*Jason*

1345  　　Loose the bolts as quickly as you can, servants,

　　　　open the doors, let me see this double evil,

　　　　them dead and her...I'll make her pay for it.[67]

[*Medea appears above the house in a chariot drawn by dragons.*[68]]

　　　　*Medea*

　　　　Why are you trying to force these doors,

　　　　seeking the corpses and me, who made them?

　　　　Save your efforts.  If you have need of me,

　　　　if you want something, say it, but your hand

1350  　　will never touch me.  My grandfather

　　　　the Sun is giving me this chariot,

　　　　for protection against hostile hands.

　　　　*Jason*

1355  　　O hate!  O most utterly hateful woman—

　　　　to me and the gods and the whole race of man,

　　　　who dared to put to the sword your children,

　　　　that you bore, destroying me and leaving me

　　　　childless.  How can you still look on the sun

　　　　and earth after you've done this, dared this most

　　　　impious deed?  You should die!  I know now

1360  　　what I didn't know then, when I brought you

[67]*The Greek audience would now expect the doors of the house to open and the children's bodies to be rolled out on the ekkyklema (wheeled platform); instead, Medea swoops down in her supernatural chariot in a kind of* deus ex machina.*

[68]*Medea's appearance in the crane symbolizes her more-than-human status: she has almost become a goddess. Her triumph over Jason is complete and obvious, as she is literally towering above him.*

from your home and barbarian land
to a Greek home, a great evil, betrayer
of your father and the land that nurtured you.
The gods sent your avenging demon against me,
for you killed your own brother at the hearth
1365 and then you boarded my beautiful ship,
the Argo. You started like this, but then,
after becoming this man's bride and bearing
his children, for the sake of your empty bed,
you killed them! No Greek woman would dare to do this,
1370 but I didn't choose them; I decided
to marry you, a hateful and destructive
cause of sorrow to me, a lioness,
not a woman, like Etruscan Scylla![69]
Oh—I could not sting you with ten thousand
1375 reproaches, you were born with such confidence.
Go, evildoer, polluted with our sons' blood;
all I can do is bewail my fate.
I will get no benefit from my new
marriage; I won't ever address the sons
1380 I begot and brought up—I'm ruined.

**Medea**
I could answer you with a long reply,
but Father Zeus already knows what you've
suffered from me and what I have done.
After dishonoring my bed, you weren't
1385 about to live a happy life, laughing at me,
nor the princess; nor would he who made the match,
Creon, exile me from his land unpunished.
For this, if you wish, call me a lionness,
or Scylla who lives on the Etruscan land.
1390 I've snatched your heart as was necessary.

**Jason**
You also should grieve and share these evils.

**Medea**
True; but pain is profit, if you're not the source.

[69]*a well-known monster of Greek mythology; a woman with dogs' heads emerging from her waist, who devoured sailors who passed too close to her rock*

*Jason*

1395    O children, what an evil mother you got!

*Medea*

   O sons, you perished for your father's disease!

*Jason*

   It wasn't my right hand that destroyed them!

*Medea*

   But it was your insult and new marriage.

*Jason*

   You really thought they should die for your bed?

*Medea*

1400    Do you think this is a small pain for a woman?

*Jason*

   If she's sensible, but nothing is good for you.

*Medea*

   They are dead, because it will hurt you.

*Jason*

   They are, alas, pollution on your head.

*Medea*

   The gods know who began the sorrow.

*Jason*

1405    They also know your disgusting mind.

*Medea*

   Hate me!  I hate your bitter speechifying.

*Jason*

   And I yours!  But ending it is easy!

**Medea**

How then?  What should I do?  I certainly want that.

**Jason**

Allow me to bury and mourn these corpses.

**Medea**

1410     Never!  I myself will bury them with this
        very hand.  I will take them to the temple
        of Hera on the mountain, so that none
        of my enemies can dig up the tomb
        and insult them; and I enjoin upon this
        land of Sisyphus a solemn festival
        and rites for all time in expiation
1415     of this impious murder.[70] I myself
        am going to the land of Erechtheus,
        to live with Aegeus, son of Pandion;
        while you are going to die a bad death,
        a fitting end for a wicked man,
1420     struck on your head by a piece of the Argo,
        having seen the bitter end of my marriage.[71]

**Jason**

Then may our children's Fury destroy you—
and murderous Justice!

1425 **Medea**

What god or spirit listens to you,
the oath-breaker and deceiver of friends?

**Jason**

Oh, oh, foul, child-murdering woman!

**Medea**

Go home and bury your wife.

1430 **Jason**

I will, unlucky in both my children.

[70]*There was actually a ritual in Corinth relating to the murders of the children; see* Mythology, *page 65*

[71]*This is the standard myth of Jason's death.*

*Medea*
Don't mourn yet; wait for your lonely old age.

*Jason*
O dearest children!

*Medea*
           To their mother, yes, but not to you.

*Jason*
And still you slew them?

*Medea*
1435            To cause you pain.

*Jason*
Alas, this poor man longs to kiss
the dear mouths of his children!

*Medea*
Now you would address them, now you would kiss
      them,
but then you pushed them away.

1440 *Jason*
           By the gods, let me
touch the soft skin of my children!

*Medea*
Impossible; your words are spent in vain.

           [*Exit Medea in the chariot.*]

*Jason*
Zeus, do you hear how I am driven away
and what I suffer at the hands of this accursed woman,
this child-slaying lioness?
1445   Only this much is possible: I can
mourn and call upon the gods,
calling heaven to witness how
you killed my children and then prevented me

from touching them and burying their corpses,
1450    whom I would never have sired
to see them dead by your hands.

*Chorus*

Zeus dispenses many things from Olympus,
and the gods bring to pass much that is unexpected.
What was believed is not borne out,
1455    while God finds a way for the unforeseen.
So it was in what has just passed.

# Mythology

Greek tragedies were almost always based on well-known stories, so that just by hearing the names of the characters, the audience would already know a good deal about the play they were about to see. The story of Jason's adventures with the Argonauts was one of the most well-known myths of ancient Greece, even though it was not written as an epic until centuries after Euripides, in the *Argonautica* of Apollonius of Rhodes.

The tale is set two generations before the Trojan War, the setting of Homer's *Iliad* and the most famous epic of ancient Greece. Jason was a prince and rightful heir to the kingdom of Iolcus, but he was raised in ignorance of his royal roots and had to battle with his uncle Pelias, who had seized the throne. Pelias sent Jason on a quest to recapture the Golden Fleece, a solid gold sheep skin from a mythical golden ram. The Fleece was in the faraway kingdom of Colchis, a barbarian land on the Black Sea. To reach this distant land, Jason was aided by his patron goddesses Hera, the queen of the gods, and Athena, goddess of wisdom and crafts, who helped Jason build the first ship, the *Argo*.

Jason assembled a group of heroes from all over Greece to sail with him in the *Argo*. The Argonauts (the word combines the name of the ship with the Greek word for "sailor") included Heracles, the greatest hero of Greece, and Castor and Pollux, the sons of Zeus and brothers of Helen of Troy. They had many adventures on their way there; the most perilous was the voyage through the Symplegades. At the entrance to the Black Sea (the modern Dardanelles in Turkey), according to this myth, there were two rocks which crashed together whenever anything passed through them. Athena, however, helped the *Argo* to sail through, and the rocks never crashed together again, thus opening the Black Sea and the barbarian lands beyond to the Greeks.

Upon the Argonauts' arrival in Colchis, the king assigned a number of tasks to Jason, such as yoking fire-breathing bulls and sowing a field with dragon's teeth, which instantly grew into armed and angry soldiers. Jason was at a loss, until the king's daughter, the skilled witch Medea, fell in love with him and came to his aid.

Medea then helped Jason to lure the Golden Fleece from the dragon who guarded it; in most versions, she drugged the dragon so that it fell asleep. In order to escape from Colchis, Medea murdered her brother and chopped his body to pieces, which she scattered from the *Argo*. Because a corpse had to be buried for that soul to find peace in the afterlife, Medea's father gave up the pursuit of Jason so that he could gather the parts of his son and bury them. Medea fled with Jason and married him.

Even though Jason brought the Golden Fleece back to Iolcus, Pelias refused to give him the kingship. Medea used her witchcraft to trick Pelias' daughters. She cut up an old ram, threw it into her cauldron, and produced a living lamb in its place. She told Pelias' daughters that they could rejuvenate their old father in the same way, but, of course, all they did was butcher and boil him. Forced to flee Iolcus, Jason, Medea, and their children eventually came to Corinth, which is where Euripides' play takes place.

As for the events that occur at the end of the play, there actually was a ritual in Corinth relating to the murdered children of Medea, though the standard explanation was that the Corinthians had murdered them in revenge after Medea killed the king and princess. It makes much more sense for the Corinthians to perform rituals to rid themselves of their own guilt—one reason why scholars suspect that Medea's murder of the children herself is a Euripidean invention, with these instructions by the now semi-divine woman as an explanation to link the two stories together.

# Greek Tragedy: An Overview

## The Genre of Greek Tragedy

The Greek tragedies that survive for us today were written and performed in a specific setting: the democratic city of Athens in the 5th century. They owe their literary background to the epic poems of Homer, the *Iliad* and *Odyssey,* as well as lyric poems performed by large choruses, often on mythological subjects.

Greek legend attributed to Thespis the invention of acting (hence, we call actors "thespians"). Drama was born when, instead of just narrating events, an actor assumed a character and interacted accordingly with the chorus, which consisted of a group of people specific to the drama (hence, in *Medea,* the chorus is made up of women of Corinth). Both actor and chorus performed wearing elaborate costumes and masks. According to Aristotle, the great playwright Aeschylus added the second actor and Sophocles the third. With these three actors playing multiple roles (by changing their masks backstage), a complete story could be acted out, and gradually the role of the chorus diminished. In the plays of Euripides, the chorus rarely achieves the role of a real character as it so often does, for instance, in the plays of Aeschylus.

The plays followed a fairly strict structure, with a prologue, the entrance of the chorus, and then several episodes separated by choral odes. The dialogue of the plays is written in meter, but was spoken, like the plays of Shakespeare, whereas the choral odes were written in a more complicated meter for the chorus to sing and dance. The plays also include a *kommos*, in which the main character(s) lament in song with the chorus. All in all, the form of Greek tragedy occupies a place somewhere between Shakespeare and opera. It is important, all the same, for modern readers to remember that they are getting a small portion of what the original audience received, for they are reading a *libretto* without the benefit of any music or the often elaborate costumes and scenery.

# Tragedy and the City

The genre of tragedy is the particular product of the Athenian democracy. In the late 6th century BCE, the Athenians drove out the family of tyrants who had ruled the city for decades and established the only true democracy in western history. Almost all political offices were chosen by lot, and the assembly of all Athenian citizens voted directly on all important issues. It was during the 5th century that Athens became the most powerful city of Greece. After joining with other Greek cities to repel an invasion by the Persian Empire, the largest empire in the world at the time, Athens became an imperial power herself, conquering other Greek cities and eventually stretching her power too far and collapsing. Sparta and her allies conquered Athens in 404, and, although the democracy was restored and continued throughout the 4th century, Athens would never regain the glory she had achieved a century earlier.

Fifth-century Athens saw an almost unparalleled cultural achievement, with enlightenment extending from philosophy and science through architecture and the visual arts. Tragedy was the premiere literary genre of this period, and it is fitting that the apex of the democracy should be symbolized by a genre of poetry that involves the entire citizen body. Performed at one of the major festivals of the city, the Great Dionysia, each tragedy was part of a contest. Three playwrights would be chosen by a city official, and each playwright would produce three tragedies and a satyr-play (a kind of farce intended to lighten the mood after three tragedies), all four plays being performed in a single day. The audience consisted of about 15,000 citizens, and the festival itself became a pageant of Athenian power and glory.

We know of many playwrights from this century, but the works of only three survived the end of antiquity and the Middle Ages, in which so much of ancient literature was lost. Fortunately, the three poets we have were universally considered to be the best: Aeschylus, Sophocles, and Euripides. Of these three, Euripides won many fewer victories that the other two; he won the first prize only four times, compared to the thirteen victories of Aeschylus and the twenty of Sophocles. Nevertheless, Euripides was considered during his life to be one of the greatest playwrights; he was also extraordinarily popular after his death, both in Athens and beyond. As a result, more of his plays than those by Aeschylus and Sophocles have survived. The major surviving plays of Euripides besides *Medea* include *The Bacchae, The Trojan Women, Hippolytus,* and *Iphigenia in Aulis. Medea* was part of a tetralogy (group of four plays) that came in third at the festival. Does this tell us that the Athenians did not like the play? Remember that prizes were awarded for all four plays as a group. Without knowing the quality of the plays that accompanied *Medea*, we cannot know exactly why it came in third, although the play's dark, controversial nature has led many scholars to believe that it may have offended the conventional sensibilities of the judges.

*Medea* was first performed in 431 BC, a time when Athens was at the height of her power, and although plague would wreak havoc on the city, Athenians could view their empire and the war with Sparta with confidence. It was also a period when Sophocles was the dominant figure of tragedy and had already produced classic plays like *Antigone*. Euripides was well established, as well, however, and had won his first victory in 441 BC.

## Conventions of Greek Drama

The most important convention of the Greek stage was the wearing of masks with attached wigs by all performers. As such, facial expression, which plays so large a role in modern theater, was not a factor. Additionally, the elaborate costumes worn by the actors and chorus members were often the most striking visual element. Staging was usually limited to the painted background behind the stage. Greek tragedies are all set outside, so this background usually depicted the exterior of the main characters' residence—in *Medea's* case, the house of Medea in Corinth. Changes of scene are rare in Greek tragedy, and props are kept to a minimum. The action of the drama takes place over a single day. In addition to the chorus and the three actors, mute characters could also appear on stage as needed, and important people like Jason and Medea would almost always appear with attendants. In front of the stage proper, which was not raised from the ground as in modern theaters, was a circular area called the *orchestra*, in which the chorus performed its dances. These would have musical accompaniment provided by an *aulos,* a double pipe similar to a modern oboe.

While ancient technology did not allow much in the way of special effects, there were two devices that Athenian playwrights could use to add great spectacle to their staging. One was a device called the *ekkyklema*. Since the action of the play takes place outside, the *ekkyklema* revealed the inside of the house. The stage doors would be thrust open and the *ekkyklema* would roll out, almost always carrying the corpses of characters who had just been killed inside. This happened so often in Greek tragedy that it would be expected by the audience; watch carefully to see how Euripides plays with this expectation in *Medea*.

The other stage effect was a crane known simply as the machine, which allowed characters to fly above the house and which usually provided striking entrances for gods. Mortal characters almost never appeared with the machine, and Euripides in particular often ended his plays by having a god or other divine character appear via the machine and straighten out a situation that was too confused or terrible for mortals to solve themselves. This is where we get the phrase *deus ex machina*, "the god from the machine," referring to a plot device solving a story's problems with an element from outside the text itself.

# Glossary

**agon:** part of a Greek drama in which two characters offer long speeches with sophisticated rhetorical devices, as if they were opponents in a law court; in between speeches, the Chorus leader offers a few lines, usually impartial and removed from the situation, to emphasize their lesser emotional involvement in the situation. Remember that in Athens, the most radical democracy in European history, the juries who decided law cases were made up of hundreds of citizens chosen randomly, and all laws were voted on in an Assembly of at least 6,000. Every Athenian citizen (the original audience of *Medea*) would have some experience hearing speeches like this, so this was a part of a play they could understand from their own lives.

**Corinth:** one of the major cities of Greece, both in mythology and in 5th-century history; located at the Isthmus of Corinth, the land bridge between mainland Greece (where Athens was) and the Peloponnesus (the hand-shaped peninsula where Sparta, Athens' main rival, was located), Corinth had a very strategic position in controlling the movements of armies from one part of Greece to another. Corinth was also a very important sea-power. Historically, there were rites for Medea's children in Corinth, so Euripides is following tradition by placing the story there.

**deus ex machina:** literally, "the god from the machine"; Greek tragedies often end with a god appearing in a crane over the stage to sort things out, providing a neat ending with a voice that cannot be argued against.

**ecstasy:** Greek religion allowed for spiritual ecstasy, considered divine possession by a god, symptoms of which could include falling, foaming at the mouth, speaking 'in tongues,' and so forth. The disease epilepsy was considered a form of this and was called in Greek "the sacred disease."

**meter:** Dialogue in Greek tragedy is normally spoken in *iambic trimeters,* but in times of heightened emotion may be chanted or sung. When Medea first appears, for instance, she sings in *anapests*, and the nurse sings back to her. *Anapestic* meter is the normal meter for the Chorus' entrance.

**mute characters:** There would often be mute characters onstage; they are not listed in our manuscripts, and we know about them only because they are occasionally addressed by other characters. This is another reminder that, in a society accustomed to slavery, the presence of servants was almost unconsciously overlooked.

**Pittheus:** King of Troezen, a city southwest of Athens; in some versions of the Aegeus/Pittheus story, Pittheus, who understood the riddle, tricked Aegeus into sleeping with Pittheus' daughter, who subsequently bore Aegeus' son Theseus, the great hero and king of Athens. Euripides does not say that he is following this story, but it would make the comments about Pittheus' character quite ironic.

**supplication:** A *suppliant* (person making a request from a position of powerlessness) would often grasp the knees of a person being beseeched, and might also touch the person's beard or chin.

At the knees were thought to have a direct line to the heart, but more importantly, grasping the knees put the suppliant in a physical position below the person considering the request. At the same time, the embrace was a symbolic "binding" of the beseeched to his or her promise. According to Greek religious thought, it was not right to refuse a request made by a suppliant in this position if the request was at all reasonable.

# Vocabulary

**antistrophe**—the part of a choral ode or kommos following the strophe; metrically identical to the strophe

**aulos**—a wind instrument that accompanied the chorus

**chorus**—a group of characters who act as a collective; in *Medea*, they are old women of Corinth.

**episode**—the part of a Greek drama that takes place between the odes; spoken rather than sung

**epode**—the part of a choral ode that follows the strophe and antistrophe

**kommos**—a lyric song sung by dramatic characters and the chorus together, usually at a point of heightened emotion

**lyric**—poetry meant to be sung

**meter**—the rhythmic division of lines in poetry

**ode**—a sung piece between episodes consisting of matched lyric stanzas; also called a stasimon

**oracle**—a holy place where gods pronounced the future or divine will to mortals; the person through whom the gods spoke these pronouncements; a pronouncement itself

**orchestra**—the round circle in front of the stage where the chorus danced

**parodos**—the first entrance of the chorus

**prologue**—the part of the tragedy before the chorus enters

**stasimon**—the Greek term for ode; takes place between dramatic episodes, allowing the chorus to reflect on the action and dialogue that has preceded

**strophe**—the first part of a choral ode or kommos

**tragedy**—a dramatic genre, loftier and more serious than comedy, often with a sad ending